Dedicated to Paul Whiteman

RHAPSODY IN BLUE™

by George Gershwin

FOREWORD

It was a while George Gershwin was putting the finishing touches on the score of "Sweet Little Devil" back in 1923, just prior to its Boston opening, that Paul Whiteman asked him to compose "something" for his epoch-making concert of symphonic jazz at Aeolian Hall on Lincoln's Birthday 1924. Gershwin, at the moment, was against it and, indeed, had almost forgotten about it were it not for the shock of learning from an item in the New York Herald-Tribune early in 1924 that he, Gershwin, was busy on a symphony for the much heralded Whiteman concert.

Here indeed was a challenge which could only be answered by "doing something about it." The symphony idea was definitely out. Gershwin originally thought of doing a conventional "blues" and let it go at that, but he realized that something more important was at stake and promptly set to work with a purpose. He decided to aim what he wrote at a misconception regarding the inflexibility of jazz rhythms. He worked the composition out in his mind and in three weeks turned out the *Rhapsody in Blue.*

The famous Whiteman concert which gave the *Rhapsody* to the world is now a matter of history. The concert itself proved conclusively that genius and artistry existed and flourished in Tin Pan Alley. The *Rhapsody* proved to be the cornerstone of what has now become a type of music thoroughly divorced from European influence and formalism, and magnificently American. So far as Gershwin was concerned, the *Rhapsody* merely proved his point—jazz was not confined to strict rhythm!

Gershwin composed the *Rhapsody in Blue* for Piano and Jazz Band. Ferde Grofé, the brilliant innovator in orchestration for the Whiteman band scored the *Rhapsody* for the following instrumentation: *8 Violins, 2 String Basses, Banjo, 2 Trumpets, 2 Trombones, 2 Pianos, Drum, 3 Saxophones* and *2 Horns.* With such an instrumentation, nearly every player "doubled" on some other instrument or instruments other than his principal one. This then, was the first available score of the *Rhapsody.* As demand for performances increased, it became necessary to, in a measure, recast the score, though retaining its original intent, but permitting the standardization of the instrumentation in such fashion that concert orchestras could cope with the work. This Grofé accomplished with much skill so that balance and color was maintained. It was not long however, before the *Rhapsody* found its way into the standard symphonic literature. Again Grofé was consulted, but rather than recast the entire instrumentation for one of symphonic proportions, Grofé cautiously and wisely added only such instrumental voices as would provide greater clarity and brilliance, still retaining *in toto* the original instrumental concept.

The greatness of the score as of the composition is in the sheer power of its inspiration. Condemnation through structural faults failed to deter the immense popularity of the work which holds its own with undiminished strength in an orchestral repertoire for which, after all, it was not written.

Rhapsody In Blue

GEORGE GERSHWIN tm

p
Moderato assai
mf tranquillo
f
mp poco scherzando
legato
pochissimo rall.

a tempo
ten.
ten.
ten.
p
R.H.
f
L.H.
martellato
ff
pp
17
poco rall.
mf
Ossia
8

Ossia
tranquillo
p
f deciso
p scherzando
R.H.
Poco agitato
p poco cresc.
mf

cresc.
f

ff molto marcato
Tempo giusto
ff
f
3

p
R.H.
R.H.
f
cresc.
sff
mf marc.
R.H.

8
R.H.
8
p
cresc.
R.H.
L.H.
f
sfz

cresc.
sfz
L.H. rall.
a tempo
ff

*) Cut may be made to *) page 16

p
poco a poco cresc.
8
L.H.
rall. e dim.
Meno mosso e poco scherzando
(Slower)
p L.H.
espr.
pp
8

8
rit.
p
p
R.H.

8
8
8
p
8

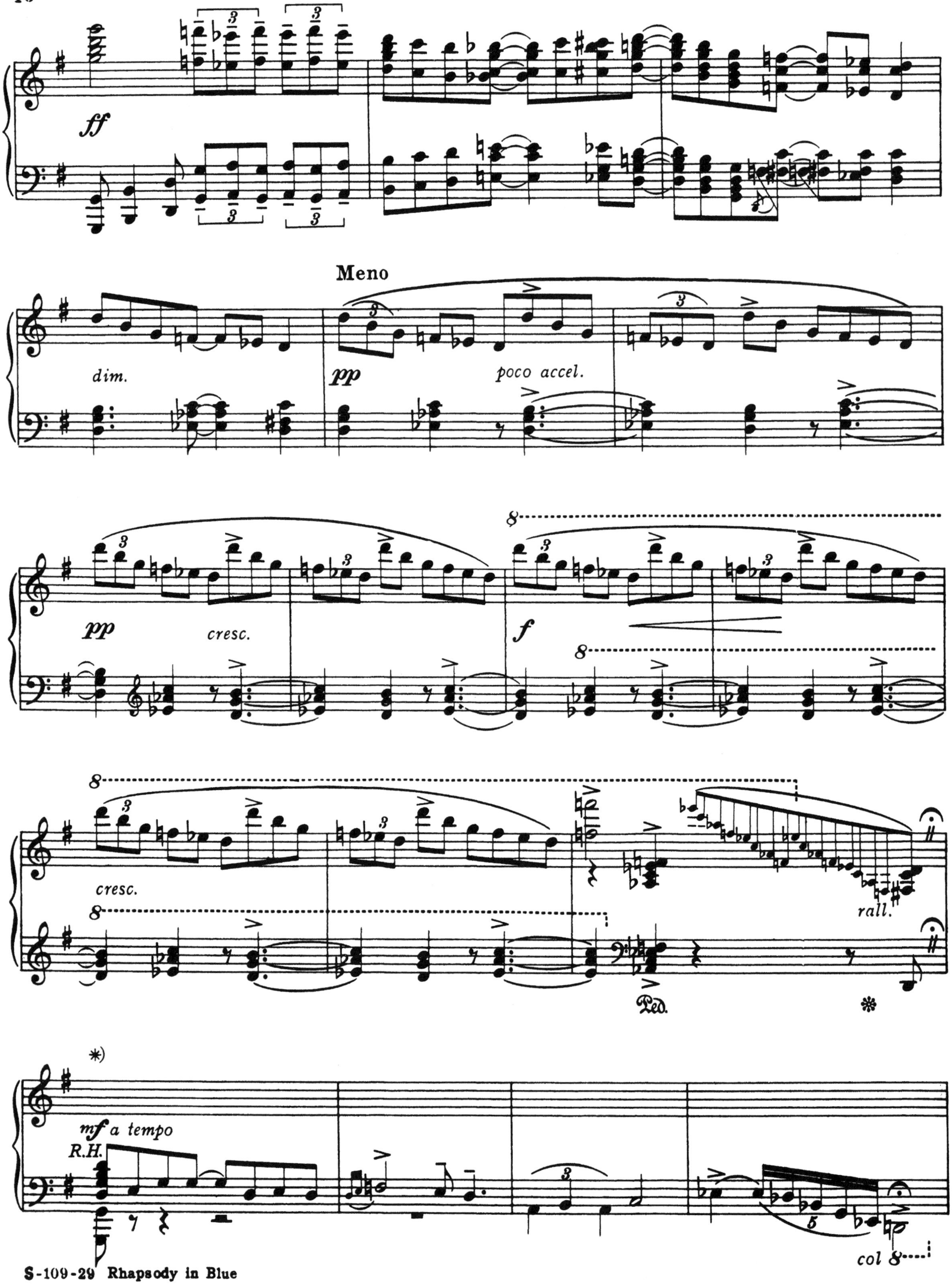
ff
Meno
dim.
pp
poco accel.
pp
cresc.
f
8
8
cresc.
8
rall.
Ped.
*)
mf a tempo
R.H.
col 8

L.H.
p a tempo
R.H.
R.H.
R.H.

R.H.
poco rall.
L.H.
p a tempo
L.H.
molto cresc.
ff
agitato
3
3
p a tempo

cresc.
martellato
ff agitato
simile
fff
Cad.
L.H.
brillante
sf

rubato e legato
pp
rall.
pp
Andantino moderato
con espressione
p
R.H.
mf
3
3

p
rit.
f a tempo
leggiero
cresc. ed accel.
ff allargando

*) May be cut to *) page 23

mf espr.
calmato

Leggiero
R.H.
L.H.
f assai staccato
p

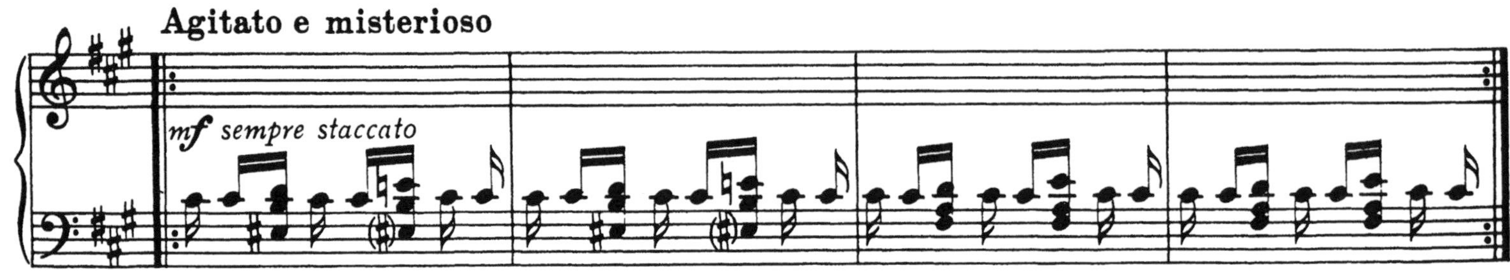
Agitato e misterioso
mf sempre staccato

L.H.
Sognando
rall. e dim.
mf a tempo

L.H.
3
3
8
f
col 8
R.H.
glissando brillante
8
p
L.H.
8
L.H.
8
poco a poco cresc.
brillante
L.H.

8
Molto stentando
ff
simile

p agitato
poco a poco cresc.

8
8
8
R.H.
Grandioso
ff marcato

8
8
poco a poco rit.

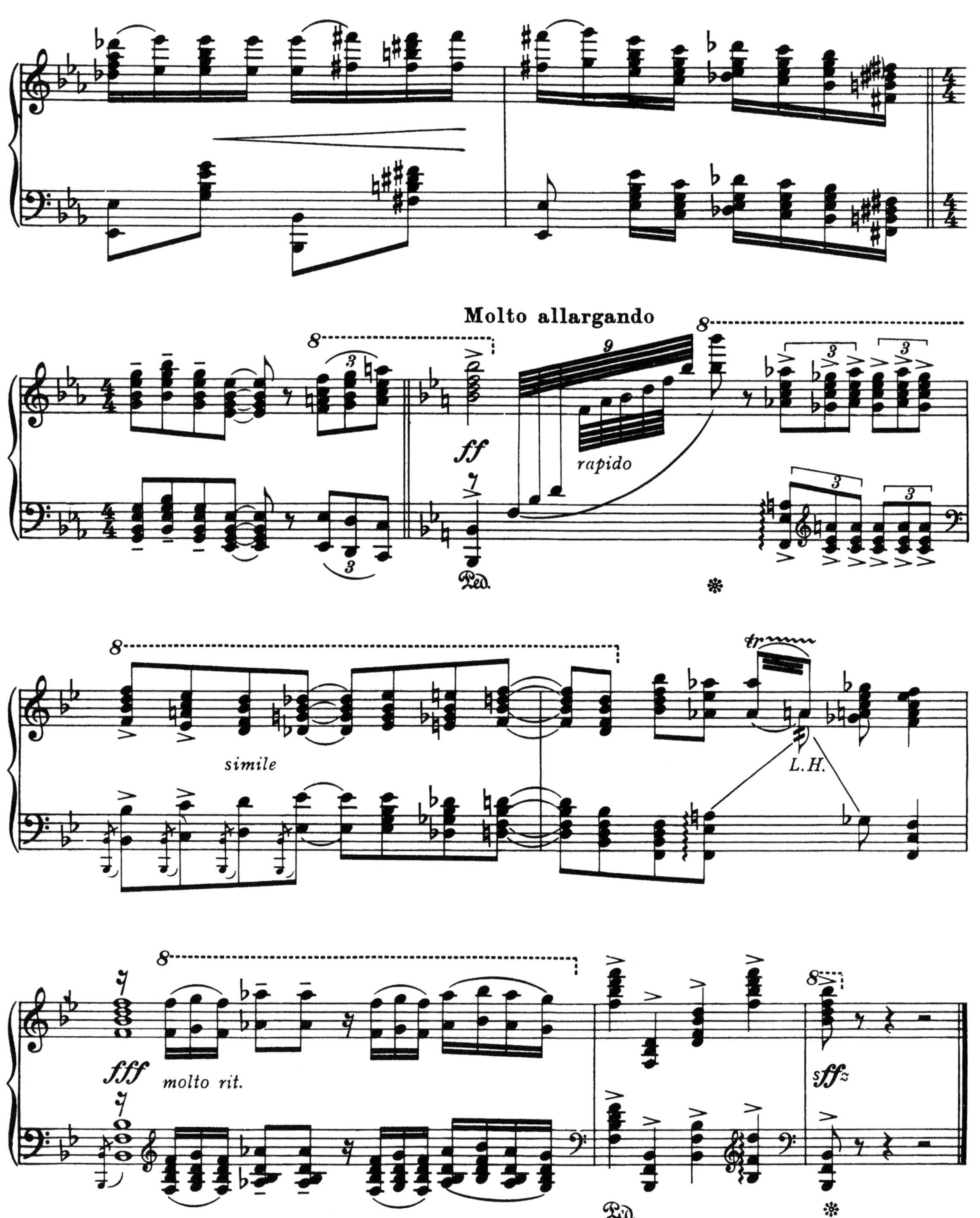
Molto allargando
ff
rapido
simile
L.H.
fff
molto rit.
sffz

Major Works of GEORGE GERSHWIN® Arranged for P★I★A★N★O

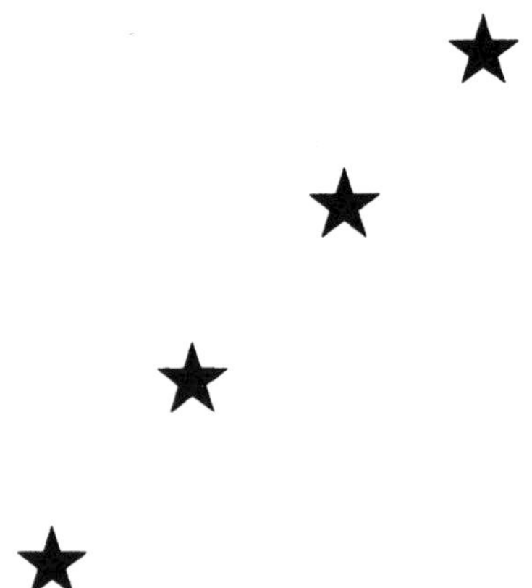

RHAPSODY IN BLUE ™

Piano Solo (based on original) (PS0047)
Piano Solo—Modified Version by Herman Wasserman (PS0048)
Piano Duet—Transcribed by Henry Levine (PS0157)
†Two Pianos-Four Hands (original setting) (PS0165)

AN AMERICAN IN PARIS ™

Piano Solo in Miniature—Transcribed by Maurice C. Whitney (PS0004)
Piano Solo—Transcribed by William Daly (PS0003)

CONCERTO IN F

Piano Solo—Transcribed by Grace Castagnetta (PS0017)
†Two Pianos-Four Hands (PS0161)

PRELUDES

Piano Solo (original setting) (PS0043)
Piano Duet—Transcribed by Gregory Stone (PS0156)
Two Pianos-Four Hands—Transcribed by Gregory Stone (PS0164)

CUBAN OVERTURE

Two Pianos-Four Hands—Transcribed by Gregory Stone (PS0162)

SECOND RHAPSODY

†Two Pianos-Four Hands (original setting) (PS0166)

†For Piano and Orchestra; Orchestral part in reduction for second piano. Two copies necessary for performance.